KU-408-087

This book belongs to:

....

DREAM
JOURNAL

ROCKPOOL
PUBLISHING

Welcome

I am fascinated by dreams and dreaming, and given that you have been drawn to this journal it looks like you are too. Did you know that we all dream? And yet, so few of us really take the time to remember or record our dreams. Even fewer apply those dreams to everyday life and to our wishful 'day' dreams so that we can transform our thinking and actions in a way that benefits us.

This journal is an opportunity to dialogue with your subconscious and bring your dreams into awareness. When you go on a fabulous and exotic trip, what do you tell your friends on your return? 'You'll never believe where I've been; the strange people I've met and the most amazing adventures that are impossible to explain!' It's the same with dreams. It's a journey into the unknown corners of your mind. In the same way you share adventures of your trip, share the details of your dreams – record them on paper or voice recording, capture the emotional intensity with images and words and let it filter into your everyday world.

I have a passion for dreams. And so I wanted to create more than just a journal where you can record them. I want to bring inspiration as well as real meaning to those random scenes in our dreams that we can only occasionally recall – and usually at times when our dreams frighten or disturb us.

This journal will guide you to understanding more about your dreams and for you to embrace the dream's messages with all its emotional intensity. Understanding your dreams' messages can allow you to heal old wounds, be open to receive and give forgiveness, practise gratitude, take a leap of faith, love more deeply and become transformed like the butterfly on the cover.

Any type of self-reflection will bring awareness of the unconscious parts of ourselves. The moment you realise that you have made new choices and decisions as a result of understanding your dream messages, that is a moment of magic. It is when you transform.

And if we truly want to make changes to our lives, we must be brave enough to confront those monsters that chase us in dreams and trap us in corners. We must learn to emerge from our cocoon of darkness and lethargy and fly high, unafraid to show our beauty and talents.

Journey and Transformation help to bring wisdom into our lives. Love is the greatest human emotion in existence, and when we find it (in whatever shape or form) we have to be thankful. The more Gratitude we have, the more love we invite into our lives.

By making this conscious decision to explore your dreaming world, you've decided to open up to its messages and to welcome dream insights into your waking day.

We are separated from our dreams by a thin veil. By lifting that veil, those changes in us that we've been wanting to make but were afraid to can finally be realised.

Be bold. Be brave. Live out your dreams. Enjoy the journey. Be transformed.

About Dreams

Dreams are a goldmine of information shedding light on what is bothering you in your waking life, and on ways to overcome your fears. For centuries people believed in the power of dreams to heal, offer spiritual insight, tell the future and solve daily problems. Many inventors have dreamed amazing ideas and solutions, as have artists, musicians and writers.

It's important to understand that dreams reflect our innermost thoughts and feelings, and our interpretation of everything that happens in our dreams is unique to us. What is most important, however, are the emotions associated with the dream. Dreams reveal feelings that need to be dealt with. There are many layers of meaning from the symbols and images in your dreams. As dreams are a reflection of your inner world, it's essential that you, and only you, are the final authority on what your dreams mean.

Recurring dreams and nightmares demand more attention. Sometimes they are quite frightening or disturbing. If you have the same dream repeatedly, your subconscious is trying to send you a message. If you make the time to think about how the dream relates to your life, you can take steps to deal with the problem.

Sometimes the events and emotions you experience in dreams have opposite meanings to those in real life. Dreams of death, for example, are not about anyone dying but are more to do with 'endings'—which then allow for new beginnings. So it's a good thing to dream of death, no matter how painful it is in the dream.

For some people who are very intuitive, precognitive dreams may foresee future events. It's common for people of all cultures, all over the world, to dream of an earthquake before it happens. It's called the 'collective unconscious' and we all have it - but we don't all access it.

Take the opportunity to dialogue with your inner self – your dreaming soul – that longs to speak to you through its metaphoric and mostly illogical dream scenarios. Honour those messages and record them in this personal dream journal.

Dream your dreams forward and carry their insights and messages into your waking world.

Sweet dreams!

How to Use Your Journal

So how do you make sense of your dreams when they appear in symbols – like some crazy encryption that doesn't make sense? The dream's message is either misunderstood or ignored when it reaches our waking brain (consciousness). But if you can work out the code and understand the symbols, you'll be grateful for the insight you get.

I've created this dream journal for you to discover the messages from your subconscious and apply the insights that you gained from the dreams to your waking life, so that you can have the opportunity to live more authentically.

The four dream themes – Gratitude, Journey, Love and Transformation– have been adopted from my *Dream Reading Cards* deck. They serve to inspire and motivate so that dream journal entries become a more interactive way for you to connect with your dream world and apply your understanding of this world to your everyday life.

- Read and reflect on these themes and see the relevance they hold for you.

- Fill out the exercises on each theme and keep in mind that both your inner and outer life will be more connected once you make it a practice.

- Feel free to write whatever insights result from your reflections. Use the blank pages to sketch a significant dream image. For example, you may wish to create a mandala while meditating on your dream image. Draw whatever comes to mind. If you prefer to cut out images from magazines or newspapers go ahead and do this. Use music to gently bring your dream message home to you while you create.

Quotes, mantras and images have been designed for you to intuitively reflect on your dreams, while the blank pages are for you to record your dreams. Make sure you reference the dream by including the date and give it a title. The title is important because it gives your dream context and brings up images and emotions felt in that dream.

Refer to the section on 'how to record your dreams' for more information on how to break down the dream scenes. First of all, just jot down the dream as you remember it and don't worry about whether it makes sense or if your grammar or spelling is incorrect.

The dream structure template can be used as a quick reference guide. You may wish to follow it so that you are able to build a customised dream reference for comparing future and past dreams. For example, if you ticked 'recurring' or 'nightmare' regularly, you would start to see a pattern emerging and you would then take some action in working out the reason for these disturbing dreams.

Remember that dreams are personal. You are the final authority on your dreams and what they mean. Take an active role in discovering your own personal symbols and the emotions they evoke so that you are able to find a meaning that truly resonates with you.

How to Remember Your Dreams

Some people have no trouble remembering dreams while others remember their dreams only occasionally or not at all. Sleep and dreams are affected by drugs, alcohol, caffeine, medication and even certain foods, so by avoiding these you may be in a better position to remember your dreams. The fact is that we all dream and it's frustrating when we know we've had a dream and we can't recall it.

Helpful tips:

- Set a clear intention throughout the day to remember your dream and, most importantly, tell yourself you will remember before you fall asleep.

- You might want to re-read some of your previous dreams to start connecting to the subconscious imagery, or alternatively meditate on a question you'd like answered.

- Write down a question or a problem you want solved and place it under your pillow.

- The way you wake up is very important. Within five minutes of waking, fifty per cent of your dream is forgotten. Within ten minutes, ninety per cent is gone. Set a soft alarm to wake you up fifteen to twenty minutes earlier than usual, when you are still in the dream state.

- As you awaken, try to move as little as possible and try not to think right away about your upcoming day. Write down all of your dreams and images, as they can fade quickly if not recorded. Any distractions will cause the memory of your dream to disappear.

How to record and interpret your dreams:

- Before you get up, keep your eyes closed and remain completely still, focusing on the memory of the dream. Write down the dream in your dream journal by your bedside as soon as you rise. Use as many details as possible.

- Write brief descriptions of images, people, places, animals and other significant details. Ask yourself, How did I feel while I was dreaming and how did I feel when I woke up?

- Journal your dreams freely. Don't worry about grammar or whether the dream makes sense. Record your dream as you remember it.

- The emotion of the dream is the most important factor to take away with you from the dream. You don't need to analyse your dream right away; it's worth processing first and then coming back to work it out later.

Ask yourself:

- Was this dream a recurring dream or similar to one you have had before?

- Was it associated with an event (e.g. starting a new job)?

- What was going on in your personal life at this time? Think back from two weeks before the dream up until the day of the dream.

- Connect the images to specific situations in your waking life. Does the theme remind you of anything or anyone in your life or part of yourself? Find as many links as you can.

- What part did you take in the dream? Were you acting the same way as you do in real life? What about the other people in your dreams? Were they people you recognise or did they represent someone you know?

- Read through your dream journal occasionally and discover the main themes, patterns, recurrences or changes in these themes. You will gain greater meaning and insight into your waking-life issues or concerns.

Recording Your Dreams

TITLE OF DREAM:

DATE:

Record your dream using as much detail as you can. Include people, actions, animals, weather, places, environment, and other:

Type of dream:

○ Positive   ○ Disturbing   ○ Recurring   ○ Nightmar

○ Fantasy   ○ Ordinary   ○ Bizarre   ○ Other

Emotions experienced in the dream or atmosphere in the dream: (e.g. Anger, confusion, freedom, love, fear)

Review of dream:

○ Significant

○ Insignificant

○ Message Understood

○ Needs deeper interpretation

○ Other

Relevance to real life situatio and emotional issues:

○ Relationships

○ Work

○ Health

○ Values

○ Personal growth

○ Other

Gratitude

Gratitude

Focus on what you have rather than what's missing in your life. Whatever we focus on, the universe will send us. If we put our energy into being grateful, the universe will provide even more. Prosperity will flow easily into your life.

Be grateful for something every day, no matter how simple: the sun on your face, the wind in your hair, and simply for being alive. There is so much to be grateful for. Say it out loud – 'Thank you' is a powerful phrase.

Appreciate everything and everyone, even those who annoy you, for they are here to teach you. Go one day without complaining.

Now watch your dreams change as your new attitude to life filters into your dream world. Do you feel more peaceful? Do you feel more rested when you wake up? Are there positive scenes in your dreams?

Practise gratitude daily. Count your blessings. Once you do this in both the waking and dreaming world, your attitude will shift and you will feel more in sync with your life.

How Grateful Are You?

This list will help you get a feel for where you're at right now and where you want to be. Your dream world will give you an opportunity to make changes to your life and help you shine a light on the things hidden deep inside your subconscious:

Rate your gratitude scale from 1 to 10 (with a score of 1 as the lowest and 10 the highest).

	Now Date:	In 3 months Date:	In 6 months Date:	In 9 months Date:	In 12 months Date:
I express gratitude daily					
I love what I do					
I often spend time in nature and outdoors					
I have a good relationship with my partner, family and friends					
I smile daily					
I laugh daily					
I challenge myself with new experiences					

	Now Date:	In 3 months Date:	In 6 months Date:	In 9 months Date:	In 12 months Date:
I feel in control of my life					
I exercise regularly					
I spend quality time with the people close to me					
I feel optimistic					
I live in the present					
I meditate					
I live an authentic life					
I have a clear vision of my goals					
I help others					
I take care of myself and my health					
Other					

An Exercise in Gratitude

Before you go to sleep, set the intention to find gratitude in your waking life. Set the intention to find ways for your dream to support you as you work towards being thankful. You may wish to write this before you go to sleep or upon waking, especially if you've had a dream that has been significant to you – good or bad.

I am grateful for:

I am grateful because:

I release all old patterns, behaviours and belief systems that have kept me from being grateful.

They are:

_____

_____

_____

_____

I will show gratitude by:

_____

_____

_____

I promise to practise gratitude daily by:

_____

_____

_____

_____

_____

_____

Record Your Dreams

/ /

I AM GRATEFUL FOR

EVERYTHING

&

EVERYONE

IN MY LIFE

The sun *never* says
to the earth,

"*You owe me.*"

Look what happens with
a love like that. It lights
up the *whole sky*.

Hafiz

Journey

Journey

When you find yourself in a strange dreamscape, know that you are embarking on a journey to self-discovery. The destination is not known, but you are getting ready to move on and tackle the next phase of your life.

In your inner journey be prepared for some unexpected surprises, a few obstacles and lots of false starts. Your 'journey' dreams will take you to roads less travelled, where you may lose your way or perhaps be flown to breathtaking scenes in unknown regions. Take a risk and follow your journey dream. Know that you will reach your destination one way or another. Isn't that why they say that it's the journey and not the destination that is important in life?

Once your journey dream surfaces from your subconscious, prepare to try something different and step out of your comfort zone. You are now ready to do it. Being in a transitional phase in our lives brings up many opportunities to change direction in all areas – career, relationships, fears, values and more.

Monitor your dreams once you've begun to make some subtle changes to your lifestyle and attitudes. Do you feel more comfortable in certain places your dreams take you to? Are landscapes becoming more familiar? Do you find yourself feeling courageous in hostile environments?

Explore different ways to get closer to your spiritual centre. Do not go in haste. Savour the journey. Experience it slowly so that it may reveal your true destination.

Begin with a single step.

Your Personal Journey

This list will help you get a feel for where you are right now and where you want to go when it comes to following your dreams and goals. Your dream world will give you glimpses of what's possible to achieve, and retrieve those long forgotten, dusty ambitions and passions that have remained dormant inside you. Now is the time to reactivate missed opportunities, challenge your fear of failure or bad timing and reach for your dreams. A wonderful journey awaits as you step on the path to discovering yourself.

Rate your level of satisfaction in these areas on a scale from 1 to 10 (with a score of 1 as the lowest and 10 the highest).

	Now Date:	In 3 months Date:	In 6 months Date:	In 9 months Date:	In 12 months Date:
I am in the flow at work and my personal life					
I am in a job I love					
I am confident in my body					
I am healthy, energised and strong					
I have other interests outside home and work that I participate in					

	Now Date:	In 3 months Date:	In 6 months Date:	In 9 months Date:	In 12 months Date:
I try new things that I have a passion for					
I'm living a fully passionate life					
I am living in my ideal house in my ideal location					
I only have people that I want around me					
I have good and loving relationships					
I am with my ideal partner					
I have 'me' time on a regular basis					
I explore spirituality in all its forms					
I live the life I dreamt of					
Other					

An Exercise in Following Your Journey

Before you go to sleep, set the intention to ask your subconscious mind to help you find a direction that best fills your true purpose in your waking life. Have a visual example of where you want to be in your life right now – relationships, work, health, lifestyle, finance, home life – and ask your dream to support you in finding the right people and circumstances to help you achieve your vision.

Big Picture:

If I could have, be or do anything, what would it look like?

Steps I have taken to achieve goals for my future:

What are my short-term/long-term goals?

Why do I want to achieve this goal?

What is holding me back? What obstacles do I face?

Record Your Dreams

/ /

The only

JOURNEY

is the one

WITHIN

· · · · · · · · · ·

RAINER MARIA RILKE

I
AM
READY
FOR
NEW
ADVENTURES

Love

Love

It is said that love is all that matters. The mystics and divine masters were right: Research shows that happiness and life fulfilment revolves around love or searching for love. The benefits of love are numerous. Lao Tzu says: 'Being deeply loved by someone gives you strength, while loving someone deeply gives you courage.'

Love is something we strive for and something we mourn the loss of. The more you are open to love, the more your heart can feel and give freely. No matter where you are right now, love should be your compass. It will help you come home to yourself – to your inner being.

Take a risk.

Trust in love.

Live in compassionate love and approach every situation from the view of love. Everything that comes from a place of love will make a difference in the lives of those around you and help raise human consciousness.

When you experience love in your life and this potent emotion filters into your dream world – all is possible. Carry this feeling of love forward into your everyday life.

Remember that the one to love the most is you. Love will guide you home. Venture into a passionate love affair with yourself and then share that love with the world.

Love deeply and with your whole heart and watch the ripple effects around you.

Understanding Love

This list will help you understand where you are at with
your relationships and where you want to be when it comes
to inviting love in your life – whether it's family, friends or
intimate partners. Your dream world will guide you back to
your heart and give voice to your feelings in your waking life.
If you've felt disappointment in love along the way, now is the
time to forgive yourself and others and open your heart again
to what's possible. Broken hearts can be mended but only if
you trust the process. Let your dreams wash away your hurts
and begin to love again. It's time to find your way home – back
to you.

*Rate your level of satisfaction in these areas on a scale from 1 to 10 (with a score
of 1 as the lowest and 10 the highest).*

	Now Date:	In 3 months Date:	In 6 months Date:	In 9 months Date:	In 12 months Date:
have people n my life that love and who ove me					
attract ositive people n my life					
am confident nat I treat veryone with espect					
have healthy oundaries					
show love to ny partner, mily and iends					

	Now Date:	In 3 months Date:	In 6 months Date:	In 9 months Date:	In 12 months Date:
I show love for myself by having self respect and taking care of my needs					
I show support and interest in those I love					
I believe that I am worthy of love and that I attract love into my life					
I believe in the power of love to create change					
I am of service to others and give unconditional love					
I am honest and loyal					
I take responsibility for my own happiness					
Other					

An Exercise in Love

Before you go to sleep, set the intention to ask your subconscious mind to help you connect with your heart and find the emotional strength to live your life lovingly. Think about the significant people in your life – your partner, family and closest friends – and remind yourself of what it feels like when you are with them. Are the emotional ties strong? If not, consider exploring how to deepen those connections.

What's your relationship with yourself – are you self-critical or are you self-accepting? If you're looking for a new relationship, make sure you are at peace with yourself and not searching for someone to love you when you can't do that for yourself. It is not a substitute.

Ask your dreams to show you how to be more loving to others (and yourself) and invite your heart to reveal its longings to you. Then act on these longings when you wake and go out into the real world. An open heart can change the way you see the world and attract the right people in your life.

I am loving because:

I show self-love by:

I am grateful for having loving people around me. I show my appreciation by:

I am confident and self-loving when:

What I need to do first before I can look for a romantic relationship:

I have learnt these qualities from these people:
Eg. Respect – my dad

My affirmation of thanks to all people in my life who are loving and who love me:

Record Your Dreams

/ /

Except for

LOVE

nothing you see
will remain forever

~~~~~~~~

Rumi

TODAY I CLOSE THE DOOR TO THE

past

OPEN THE DOOR TO THE

future

AND START A NEW CHAPTER
IN MY LIFE

Transformation

Transformation

The wise proverb tells us that 'Just when the caterpillar thought the world was over, it became a butterfly.'

Just when we think all hope is lost and all doors are closed, you soar above your expectations. Like the butterfly, you need the strength and faith to believe that, in time, you will emerge from your cocoon. With every ending comes a new beginning. Trust and let go of what no longer serves you. Be open to new ways of being and doing.

The only constant is change. To resist change is to be oblivious to growth and refuse opportunities to become self-aware. It's time for new beginnings. Act on passions and dreams you've put on hold. Tune into your dreams that encourage you to look at yourself differently.

What are you waiting for? There's never the right time if you are waiting for life to accommodate your deepest desires. Once you change on the inside, you will attract all that is positive and good for you.

You may not think you need to change. You may not want to have to transform your life, but like the butterfly, the effort to go through the painful changes will be worth it in the end. You will emerge from the darkness of the cocoon and fly free in your new, beautiful form. It is time to begin again. Don't be afraid to take a leap of faith and embrace new opportunities.

Be transformed.

The Magic of Transformation

This list is, in fact, a measure of your authenticity and passion. The questions are designed to rate your level of living your life in the most authentic manner. Have you remained in your safe, dark cocoon, too afraid to emerge in case your vulnerability would be the end of your life as you know it? Change is universally regarded as one of the most difficult things to embrace. It's hard. Even good change is hard because we are hard-wired for the perceived safety of what we know.

Your dreams are the more reliable emotional barometer. You will know when you are resisting changes because you'll have recurring chase dreams, you'll dream that your teeth are falling out, or that you'll be running for a train, bus or plane and keep missing it. Obviously, you don't feel prepared for your life to become something new.

This is the best time to incubate dreams that come to your assistance and give you advice, find solutions and equip you emotionally to face the transformation that is about to take place. Change one thing and be ready to see how the universe will support you in taking that first step.

Become the person you've always wanted to be – but were too afraid.

Rate your level of satisfaction in these areas on a scale from 1 to 10 (with a score of 1 as the lowest and 10 the highest).

	Now Date:	In 3 months Date:	In 6 months Date:	In 9 months Date:	In 12 months Date:
I am stressed, emotionally exhausted, worried and unhappy					
I am feeling cynical and pessimistic					
I do the same things I've always done					
I feel lost and disconnected from myself and others					
I find it hard to get motivated to make changes					
I'm living the life I've designed for myself and want					
I try something new every day					
Other					

An Exercise in Transformation

At bedtime, prepare your bedroom for dreaming – soft lights, meditative music, burn your favourite oils and be ready for a dream with a difference. Whether you remember your dream or not is not important. Your subconscious mind will store the dream message and you will be able to access it when you are ready to act on the advice. Set your intention and ask your subconscious mind to help you access parts of yourself that have been long buried and need reawakening for true authenticity.

Think about living the kind of life you want and not the kind that is dictated to you by your fears, negativity, and the expectations of others.

Life is not a rehearsal. We get one shot at it. It's important that you live in harmony with your inner being and express your passions fully and without fear of judgement. Just like the butterfly, emerging from the cocoon will free you and you will at last become who you were meant to be.

When I was younger, I always wanted to:

If I could do anything or be anyone, I would:

I've started my bucket list and before my life is over I will:

I need changes in these areas of my life in order to shape a life that fits with the real me:

Obstacles that are blocking the way to unlocking my true passion, strengths, talents and gifts:

Positive qualities that make me unique in these areas - *intellectual; spiritual; physical; emotional:*

Labels I have given myself or that have been given to me by others. *How I will change these labels:*

Record Your Dreams

/ /

JOY
is not in
things
it is
in us

....

RICHARD WAGNER

My

DREAMS

shape my

REALITY

Record Your Dreams in Pictures

Use this section to draw your dreams.

More books by
Rose Inserra

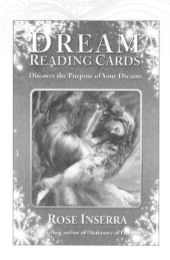

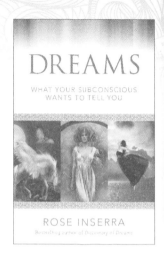

Dream Reading Cards
Rose Inserra
Beautifully illustrated cards with imagery designed to represent the major dreamlike states we all experience. Rose Inserra is the author of the *Dictionary of Dreams*, which has sold over 500 000 copies.

RRP $24.99

Dreams
Rose Inserra
Dreams is a comprehensive and practical guide to all aspects of dreaming. Discover how you can intuitively interpret your dream symbols and, on waking, use practical self-help remedies to recall the dream's message. You can learn to unlock your dreams and bring them to your conscious mind to process.

RRP $27.99

Available at all good bookstores or order online at
www.rockpoolpublishing.com.au

A Rockpool book
PO Box 252
Summer Hill
NSW 2130
Australia
www.rockpoolpublishing.com.au
http://www.facebook.com/
RockpoolPublishing

ISBN 978-1-921295-85-0

First published in 2015
Copyright text © Rose Inserra 2015
Copyright images © Rockpool Publishing 2015

Cover design by Farrah Careem
Internal design and layout by Jessica Le
All images by Shutterstock
Printed and bound in China

10 9 8 7 6 5 4 3 2 1